ELY
& DISTRICT

CHRIS JAKES

The History Press

For my mother, and in memory of my father, who
together passed on their love of this place, their
pleasure in reading, and their interest in the past.

Minster Place from the west door of the
cathedral in winter, *c.* 1900. The new public
library was built on this site, opening in 1966.

First published 1995
This edition published 2009
Reprinted 2019

The History Press
97 St George's Place, Cheltenham,
Gloucestershire, GL50 3QB
www.thehistorypress.co.uk

© Chris Jakes, 1995, 2009

The right of Chris Jakes to be identified as the Author
of this work has been asserted in accordance with the
Copyrights, Designs and Patents Act 1988.

All rights reserved. No part of this book may be reprinted
or reproduced or utilised in any form or by any electronic,
mechanical or other means, now known or hereafter invented,
including photocopying and recording, or in any information
storage or retrieval system, without the permission in writing
from the Publishers.
British Library Cataloguing in Publication Data.
A catalogue record for this book is available from the British Library.

ISBN 978 0 7524 4944 9
Typesetting and origination by The History Press
Printed in Great Britain by TJ International Ltd, Padstow, Cornwall.

CONTENTS

The unchanging image of Ely: the lopsided west front of the cathedral, seen from Palace Green. Only the costume indicates that the picture dates from a hundred years ago.

INTRODUCTION

The recorded history of Ely can be traced back to the seventh century, when the Saxon Queen Etheldreda founded a religious community here, high on an island overlooking the surrounding waterlogged and inhospitable fens. Today the successor to that community, the cathedral, dominates the city and the fenland for miles around, soaring heavenward against the backdrop of a vast open sky.

The city's prosperity has always been linked to the cathedral and to the productivity of the fenland, being both a market town and a tourist centre. The first sight of the cathedral across the flat fenland must have seemed as impressive to the medieval pilgrim as it does to the modern coach party.

It is perhaps ironic that it was during the ascendancy of Ely's most famous resident, Oliver Cromwell, that the cathedral came closest to destruction. It was only saved because it was thought that the cost of demolition would be greater than the value of the materials which could be salvaged.

Ely, it is said, has been slow to change. In 1861 the population stood at just under eight thousand. A hundred years later in 1961 it had grown to just under ten thousand. In the 1860s the principal industry was agriculture, though the manufacture of agricultural machinery, brewing, boat building, and basket making were also important. In the 1960s the principal industry was still agriculture, agricultural machinery was still being made on a large scale, the brewery served a wide area, boat building went on, and even basket making continued.

By the 1860s Ely was finally pulling itself into the nineteenth century. Scarcely a generation earlier the bishop had still been exercising spiritual and temporal power over the Isle of Ely, much as his medieval predecessors had done. Some thirty years earlier, owing to a poor water supply, one hundred and sixty people had been struck down by cholera. However, improvements did come: by the 1860s gas was lighting the streets, the railway had reached the city (1845), a new Corn Exchange had been built, a new cemetery had opened, and the water supply was being improved. Even the cathedral, which had long been neglected, was undergoing an extensive programme of restoration and refurbishment.

This period also saw the arrival in Ely of the first photographers. Some were itinerant, such as Mr Villiers, who took daguerreotype portraits from 'a portable and very convenient gallery erected on the Market hill', in May 1853. The local newspaper reported that 'the faithfulness of the likenesses is much admired, and Mr Villiers appears to be well patronised'. In the 1860 edition of his *Hand-book to the Cathedral Church . . . at Ely* T.A. Hills was advertising R. Fenton's photographic views of the cathedral, and first-class stereographs. (Coincidentally one of Fenton's views currently hangs on the waiting-room wall of a well-known Ely dental surgeon, and almost makes the visit worthwhile in itself!) In 1863 Samuel Bolton opened his photographic studio on Fore Hill.

It is the work of photographers such as these, both amateur and professional, that this volume sets out to show. It includes work by national companies such as Frith's and Valentine's, alongside that of local photographers Tom Bolton and Starr & Rignall. It also includes the work of enthusiasts who travelled the county, such as C.G.M. Hatfield, D. Reid and B. Snelson, and Ely amateur photographer Walter Lane, whose work features strongly in the postwar section.

The majority of the photographs used are from the Cambridgeshire Collection, the local studies department of Cambridge Central Library. It exists to collect, organise, and make available to the public, material relating to Cambridgeshire and the Isle of Ely. The collection also holds the photographic archive of the Cambridge Antiquarian Society, which had the foresight to actively compile a photographic buildings record for all the towns and villages in the county between the wars. Today this work is being carried on by the Cambridgeshire Local History Society, which is organising the rephotographing of the villages covered by the original survey sixty years ago.

Photographs form an invaluable part of this county's heritage, and I would appeal to all photographers, professional and amateur, and to collectors of postcards or photographs, to consider depositing copy prints or negatives of their work in one of the county's local studies collections. Time passes, memories fade, and our towns and villages are changing week by week. If you enjoy looking at 'old' photographs, consider the interest and enjoyment someone may gain from your work in twenty, fifty or a hundred years' time.

The first three sections of this book follow a broadly chronological sequence, looking at the city's life, streets and businesses during the Victorian and Edwardian periods, between the wars and in the postwar era. Sadly much of this is now passing from living memory.

Section four follows the evolution of the drainage system in the surrounding fens, upon which the prosperity of Ely has always depended. It also shows the consequences of its failure, when nature has triumphed over man's ingenuity.

The final section takes a look at the group of small villages which lie within the city boundary, but which are some 2 to 7 miles distant from the city itself. They all have their own character and sense of community, and are proud to be both separate yet part of the whole.

It is always difficult to decide what to include and what to leave out in a volume like this, and I have tried for the most part to include images not previously published. Of those which have appeared before, many are now out of print, while others are particularly fine and are worth seeing again. I hope there is something here for everyone to enjoy, for Eleans, past, present and future.

C.R.J.
Prickwillow, July 1995

Section One

VICTORIAN & EDWARDIAN ELY

A tribute first to the photographers who have recorded the life and look of Ely
over the years. Here one is surprised, and captured forever, by a colleague while
photographing the new Ely High Bridge, opened in 1910.

The cathedral dominates the city from all directions, but photographers have always preferred some aspects to others. This view from The Park is a favourite. Here it was photographed in 1872.

Just as popular is this view from the railway bridge, looking towards Annesdale Quay. This view also dates from about 1872.

Looking south from near Nutholt Lane over what was then Gaol Street. Like the previous two pictures it shows the unfinished lantern tower of the cathedral.

The lantern, complete with its surrounding pinnacles, seen from near Common Muckhill Bridge at the turn of the century.

The lantern tower before restoration, from Cross Green. The graveyard here had become so full that a new cemetery was opened off New Barns Road in 1855.

The interior of the Lady Chapel, when it was in use as Holy Trinity parish church, c. 1890.

A splendid group of clerics, displaying all the character and assurance of the Victorian Church. Their garb is reminiscent of the black habit of the Benedictine order of monks, who occupied the monastery until the Reformation.

Firmary Lane, which runs down the centre of the monastery's infirmary. The arches of the latter can be clearly seen.

A game of snowballs in The Park at the rear of The Porta, *c.* 1900. The Porta has been the home of the King's School for many years.

The Gallery from Barton Square, 1860s. The Green Man Inn is on the left opposite The Porta. Hereward Hall, opened in 1881, replaced the inn.

The Gallery takes its name from the raised walkway linking the Bishop's Palace to the south-west transept of the cathedral. The palace, seen here in 1898, was presented to the British Red Cross Society during the Second World War as a convalescent home for servicemen.

The palace library, showing part of the collection of books, furniture and paintings.

The palace and cathedral from the palace garden, *c.* 1880.

The plane tree, planted in the seventeenth century, for which the garden is famous. A gardener seems to be poised, waiting for the next leaf to fall.

The Market Place, early 1880s. Sturton & Howard, chemists, occupy the premises on the far left, and in the centre, the small single storey building in the Butter Market is occupied by Thomas Morley, butcher. In 1816 the Littleport Rioters had been tried in the Sessions House, next to the Corn Exchange.

Five of the rioters were executed on a specially constructed gallows at the Mill Pits, off what is now St John's Road. These children are bathing in the pits, 1880s.

The Market Place after the Public Room had replaced the Sessions House, *c.* 1905. As early as 1868 a meeting had been held to discuss building a public hall to house a library, museum and concert room. Market stalls can be seen in front of the Corn Exchange.

The fair comes to Ely, *c.* 1910. This is held twice a year, in May and October, for three days.

A Hospital Sunday crowd gather in the Market Place to listen to the band, 1910. Money was collected for Addenbrooke's Hospital, Cambridge.

A large crowd watches a demonstration of the new fire engine, and the Corn Exchange gets a soaking, 14 May 1912.

The shop of J. Newstead & Son, fish, poultry and game dealer, on the west side of the Market Place. John Newstead, an army veteran, was said to have 'the upright carriage and the spruce bearing of the military man'. Here his son Percy stands in the shop doorway.

When John Newstead died in 1913 some two hundred people watched the funeral procession pass along the High Street. Led by the Territorials and the City of Ely Band, the coffin was escorted by four members of his old regiment.

In the late 1880s John Wilson, saddler, occupied these premises in the Market Place, at the top of Fore Hill.

It has always been easier to walk down Fore Hill than up it. Here, on the left, is Sturton & Howard, chemists, *c.* 1905.

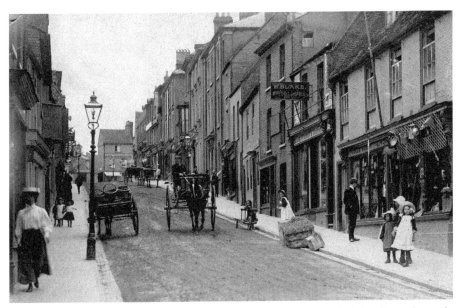

The opposite end of Fore Hill. On the right is the Constitutional Club, above the cycle agent, and next door is W. Blake, house furnisher.

Ye Olde Tea Rooms. From 1892 this restaurant and bakery was owned by the Cross family. They began to collect various items, and at the turn of the century established a folk museum in the building. The premises were sold in April 1964 and are now part of the Royal Standard public house next door. Dating from the fifteenth century, it is the oldest building on Fore Hill.

The north side of the High Street, *c.* 1905. In the foreground next to Gardiner's, the chemist, is Legge and Son, boot and shoemakers, established in 1787.

H. & J. Cutlack, on the corner of the High Street and Chequer Lane.

Opposite Cutlack in Chequer Lane stood Foster's Bank. It opened in 1835.

Later this new building was erected on the same site. In 1904 Foster's was taken over by the Capital and Counties Bank, which in turn was taken over by Lloyds in 1918.

Steeple Gate, 1870s. This is one of the gateways from the High Street (formerly Steeple Row) into the cathedral/monastic precincts. It probably dates from the sixteenth century and was built on the site of an earlier entrance. Henry Briggs, butcher, and Peter Chambers, pork butcher, were on either side of the archway. Mrs Briggs' pork pies were still commented on, in a local newspaper, sixty years later.

The Lamb Hotel, *c.* 1900. This ancient inn had prospered with the coming of the turnpike roads and coach travel.

Looking down Lynn Road from Minster Place. On the left, next to the milestone and lamp, is the Minster Temperance Hotel, which in 1900 advertised 'accommodation for commercials, tourists, and cyclists'.

Part of the crowd outside the Shire Hall and police station to hear the proclamation of King George V's accession, 12 May 1910.

Cromwell House and St Mary's Church, 1891.

Broad Street, looking north, *c.* 1910.

St Peter's Church, Broad Street, in 1891, the year after it was dedicated.

Officers of the militia, 1859. The group includes Col. Duncombe, Lt.-Col. Wale, Capt. Dickment, Capt. Fendish, Capt. Haylock, Capt. Reed, C.P. Yorke and H. Adeane.

The militia band on the parade ground off Barton Road, early 1880s. Col. Wale is behind on horseback. The militia barracks were in Silver Street.

Station Road, looking towards the level-crossing, *c*. 1905.

A train approaches the station platform, *c*. 1905.

Ely High Bridge and the station (left) from Stuntney Causeway, *c*. 1890. Compare this view with that on page 90 to see what high water meant for the traveller.

Spectators stand on the old bridge to watch the replacement being built. It opened in July 1910.

The Cutter Inn, 1880s. This took its name from the men working on the new river cut between Ely and Littleport. The licence was held at this time by the Hill family.

A solitary scull on the river near the inn. In the background, on Babylon, are cottages near Appleyard's boathouse.

Stacking osiers (willows), brought in by barge, at John Fear's rod yard, *c.* 1880.

The osiers were peeled and made into a wide variety of baskets.

The pavilion on the Paradise sports ground, *c.* 1910. This has been the arena for sports of all kinds since 1880.

The cemetery, looking towards the two chapels. The first body to be laid here was that of a Dissenter, who was buried in unconsecrated ground, in May 1855.

Pupils of Market Street Infant's School, 1891. Built in 1868 for 230 children, the average attendance was 142.

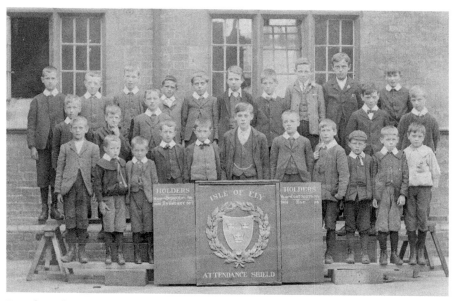

Boys from the Silver Street School pose with the Isle of Ely Attendance Shield which they won in 1909. They seem none too happy about it.

Section Two

TWO WARS & THE YEARS BETWEEN

Starr & Rignall's City Studio, on the corner of Lynn Road and St Mary's Street.

The latest wedding photographs and postcards are on display in the windows.

Wounded servicemen and staff at the former militia hospital, off Silver Street. In October 1915 it was taken over by the Ely Red Cross Voluntary Aid Detachment for the care of fourteen patients. The photograph dates from about this time.

Fortunately no one was injured when this tree crashed down on to the Palace Green during a blizzard, on 28 March 1916.

During the First World War, as the casualty list grew longer so did the desire for a commemorative shrine. This memorial in the Market Place was unveiled in June 1917.

The permanent war shrine was unveiled by Maj.-Gen. Sir S.W. Hare and dedicated by the bishop, on 30 April 1922. Ex-servicemen parade on either side of the shrine, which carries the names of 224 men.

Peace came with the armistice of 1918. In July 1919 Ely celebrated the signing of the peace treaty with a procession, dinner and sports. As the crowd leaves St Mary's Street some khaki is still visible among the civilian dress.

Part of the Peace Day procession in the High Street, showing members of the Voluntary Aid Detachment, followed by the Girl Guides and Brownies.

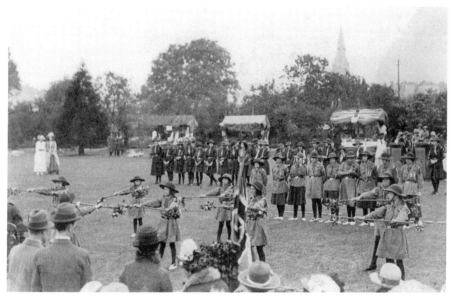

On 5 June 1920 the Ely and District Girl Guides held an Old English May Fair in the grounds of the Theological College.

Gen. Lord Horn inspects the guard of honour made up of members of the Cambridgeshire Regiment, before unveiling the county war memorial in the cathedral, 11 May 1922.

Hospital Sunday, 1922. Most of the crowd seem to be aware of the photographer in the Lamb Hotel.

The Market Place, with the jubilee fountain, 1925. Perhaps it is so quiet because it is a Tuesday or a Sunday.

Minster Place, 1925. When Lloyds Bank (centre right) was built four years earlier the Council had considered it extravagant, and, at a time of housing shortages, tried to prevent builders living within 10 miles of Ely from working on it.

The Palace Green, *c.* 1930. Schoolboys are playing in the foreground, and, as they have done for generations, some are clambering over the cannon. This was a Crimean War trophy and was placed on the green in 1860.

This and the following ten street scenes were taken by Starr & Rignall in the 1920s, and, unlike the view opposite, would probably have appealed only to Ely residents. This is Deacon's Lane, and for many years the house in the foreground stood alone on this stretch of road.

Looking from Deacon's Lane along Lynn Road. Beyond this terrace of houses lay Little London, a crowded area of cottages which had been given this name in the early part of the seventeenth century.

Egremont Street. In 1890 Fr John Freeland had come to Ely to establish a Catholic parish, and two years later a corrugated-iron chapel was erected here. It was replaced by St Etheldreda's Church in 1903. (The church is out of the picture, behind the photographer.)

Chapel Street. The chapel of the Countess of Huntingdon (a Nonconformist sect) opened here in 1793, followed by the first Methodist chapel in 1818.

West Fen Road, looking towards the corner of Hills Lane. This part of the road was formerly called Cow Lane.

Fieldside. At this time the road was a dead end, but during the 1950s and '60s it was linked to new estates.

Chiefs Lane (now Street), before the development of the eastern side.

Bernard Street, from Chiefs Street. It looks more spacious before the coming of the motor car.

Station Road, showing part of the gasworks on the right.

Back Hill, with the Royal Oak public house on the left, and the former Rifleman or Volunteer Inn opposite, on the corner of Broad Street.

Cambridge Road, looking beyond St Mary's parish room (left). At this time the street was only partially developed.

In April 1928 the new Ortona Motor Bus Company's garage was opened on Cambridge Road. The coming of the bus was said in a local newspaper editorial to have given Ely 'a new lease of life'.

A bus stands in the Market Place, opposite the Club Hotel, 1935. During the nineteenth century horse-drawn vehicles had regularly left the hotel for the surrounding villages.

Evison's fish café, the City Temperance Hotel and Sykes's, 1935. Shortly after Evison opened in 1933 he gave a free meal to some of the 'Tower House' inmates. (This was the name given by the locals to the Poor Law Institution.)

Market day, 3 April 1935. The exotically dressed fortune-teller has attracted quite an audience.

Market day, 1936. Everyone's attention is caught by what the stalls have to offer rather than by the photographer.

Buying fruit in the Butter Market. Sadly the original negative has been damaged.

The staff stand ready in the new Woolworth's bazaar, which opened on Fore Hill in the mid-1930s. The signs proudly state that there is 'nothing in these stores over 6d'.

The Woolpack Inn, on the corner of Market Street and Newnham Street, 1935. At this time the inn was kept by Walter Northrop. It closed in 1969.

Newnham Street from The Woolpack, 1935.

Wilfred Greenhill, cycle agent, Market Street, 1934. The sign advertising 'vans, fly and stage waggon' had been discovered during renovations at the beginning of 1922.

The old gaol in Market Street, 1938. This had been the bishop's prison, and was in use until 1837. The bishop had spiritual and temporal jurisdiction over the Isle of Ely and could lock up any individual who fell foul of his courts.

High Street, 1935. The spacious premises of James M. Harvey & Sons (draper's, carpet warehouse, furnisher's, etc.) dominate this part of the street. A woman stands at the entrance to High Street Passage.

A pavement artist at work in High Street Passage, March 1933.

The south side of the High Street, 1935. On the left is Barclays Bank. Next door are the premises of Russell Wright, butcher, who is advertising his 'Ely sausages'. Beyond the tree is St Audrey's, the home of Dr F.H.M.A. Beckett.

Looking through Steeple Gate into Chequer Lane, c. 1930.

King's School pupils on the school field off Barton Road. In 1939 the fees for full board and tuition were £27 a term, with 'extras kept to the lowest possible minimum'.

This monastic barn had been converted into a gymnasium and workshop by the King's School in 1921.

St Mary's Street, 1925. Bedford House, in the centre, had been home to the High School for Girls since 1905.

Girls enjoying a game of tennis at the rear of Bedford House.

Cromwell House from St Mary's churchyard, *c.* 1937. Three hundred years before, it had been the home of Oliver Cromwell.

The interior of Cromwell House, 1930. After a period as a public house, it was used as St Mary's vicarage from 1905 to 1986.

St John's Farm, showing the former chapel of St Mary's Hospital and the seventeenth-century farmhouse, *c.* 1930. The hospitals of St Mary Magdalene and St John the Baptist were medieval religious foundations for the care of the sick and poor. Originally separate, they later united. The establishment was defunct by the sixteenth century, but parts of the buildings remain.

This dovecot stood to the west of Downham Road, between West Fen Road and Upherd's Lane. It was photographed in 1914.

The Wesleyan chapel choir dressed up for a party, 2 January 1923. Back row, left to right: L. Gibbons, S. Tawn, T. Lee, W. Bullingham, H. Lemmon, L. Nash, W. Nash. Middle row: ? Hall, W. Lane, ? Morley, Mr E. Morgan, Miss E. Morgan, A. Nash, H. Morgan, ? Lane, B. Fenn. Front row: E. Ablett, A. Cooper, B. Fenn, M. Lemmon, F. McFall, W. Holland, G. Ablett, A. Dean, G. Adams, F. Sykes. The figure on the far right is Bertie Fenn.

The Theological College, Barton Square, 1920s. The college had opened in 1881, and closed in 1964.

The Board of Guardians at the Poor Law Institution, after its final meeting, March 1930. Seated in the centre is the chairman, J.C. Laxton; to his left is Miss Tuck, and behind her is F.W. Green, the clerk.

Cutlack & Harlock's Quay Brewery, looking towards Broad Street. The partnership was formed in 1912.

In 1930 Cutler & Harlock joined A. and B. Hall to become Hall, Cutlack & Harlock, the name displayed here on the Cutter Inn. The Forehill Brewery then took over all brewing.

A charming riverside
study of a cottage on
Babylon from the Quay,
1930s.

Swimmers at the bathing place on the River Ouse, 1930. The first swimming-pool was
opened on Angel Drove in 1934.

Thomas Bolton's photographic studio, Fore Hill. The Bolton family were very much involved in the history of cinema in the city. They helped to run the first purpose-built cinema, the Electric, opened in 1912, and its replacement, the Rex, opened in 1929. They also took over their rival, the Public Room.

Ex-servicemen take part in the procession to celebrate King George V's Silver Jubilee, May 1935.

In less than a year celebration turned to sadness. The king died at Sandringham, and on 23 January 1936 the royal funeral train passed through Ely. Here, men stand in silent tribute as the train approaches the city.

In May 1937 Ely celebrated the coronation of the new king, George VI. Members of the British Legion marched through the town, led by M. Johnson, seen here bearing the standard.

An indicator board erected in the Market Place, opposite the Corn Exchange, to show the amount raised during War Weapons Week, March 1941. It was designed by staff and pupils of the High School.

Members of 1094 Squadron, Air Training Corps, *c.* 1944. The group includes R. Barber, ? Catchpole, ? Crane, D. Cross, D. Dockerill, F. Hardiment, ? Hills, E. Hopkin, ? Horsley, R. Jakes, C. Leaford, A. Lee, P. Skipper, G. Tills, ? Turner and T. Utteridge.

Section Three

POSTWAR ELY

Photographers are out in force to record the visit of Princess Margaret on 21 June 1959. She took

part in the cathedral service to dedicate the Cambridgeshire Regiment's roll of honour.

Heavy snow causes problems for motorists near the Butter Market. Perhaps they should retreat to The Dolphin Inn.

Fortunately the cars at Nice's garage do not have to go anywhere. The name Cass still appears on the building. He was the first motor engineer in Ely, having started his business in 1905. In 1937 he opened another garage further along St Mary's Street, some years after this one had been taken over by T.H. Nice.

Disaster struck St Mary's Street and Nice's garage, when a Harvard two-seater trainer aircraft crashed on the morning of 9 August 1951. It hit and demolished the top of Brand's forge, careered across the street, hitting a lorry, and then plunged into Nice's showroom.

Wreckage from the plane. The driver of the lorry was killed instantly, and although the cadet and instructor were rescued the latter died in the RAF hospital.

Staff working in the St Martin factory on Bray's Lane, packing jams and marmalade. The factory operated until 1959.

J.W. Haylock's shoe shop on the corner of the Market Place at the top of Fore Hill. The buildings on the left have been replaced by the Tesco's store, which opened in 1966.

Walter Lane, the manager of Foster Brothers, took this photograph of customers queueing up for bargains in the sale. The premises had previously been occupied by W. McFall; Foster's moved here in 1933.

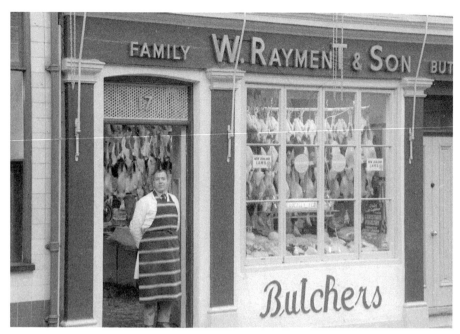

Tony Rayment at the family butcher's on Fore Hill. The shop is full of birds for Christmas.

Coronation Parade, in the High Street, May 1950. Pictured are Peacocks Stores, Kays, Bata and Finlay & Co. All these stores have now gone.

Anyone who has travelled on an Ely bus in the last forty years will recognise someone here. Eastern Counties Omnibus Co. staff are pictured at the Cambridge Road garage. The red buses of Eastern Counties had taken over from the green of Ortona in 1931.

The perils of living in St Mary's Street before the bypass opened! This articulated lorry spectacularly failed to negotiate the Cambridge Road corner. The bypass was officially opened on 24 June 1986.

The Market Place and Market Street, *c.* 1950. On the left are M.J. Russell and Kempton & Son. In Market Street are Bennett's, the Rex cinema, Olive Curtis, the Co-op, H. Sykes, Mavis Rose and the White Hart Hotel.

Awnings and summer frocks are out in Fore Hill, *c.* 1950. The bicycle was still a popular mode of transport.

The Market Place, *c.* 1951. On the shrine the plaques to commemorate the Second World War had been unveiled in November 1948. The buildings on the west side of the Market Place are occupied by Fisher & Co. and Brunning's. The Public Room Cinema is showing *Too Young to Kiss*, starring June Allyson. To the right are two posters for the Rex; one is advertising *Lullaby of Broadway*, with Doris Day.

There are advantages for the photographer in having a 215 ft high vantage point in the west tower of the cathedral. This view looks north-east over the Market Place, Cattle Market and jam factory. In the distance is the sugar-beet factory.

Looking west over St Mary's Church and St Mary's Street, towards Chiefs Street. In the distance are Debden Green and St Ovin's Green.

Looking south towards Barton Square, Silver Street, Barton Farm and the fenland beyond.

Looking north-west over Bedford House, Chapel Street, Downham Road, towards the army camp off West Fen Road.

Finally, looking north along Lynn Road, over Market Street and the Grange.

An aerial view with a difference: Back Hill, presumably from the gasworks. There are no prizes for guessing on which day of the week this was taken!

A prize-winning dive? Trophies await the competitors in the swimming club's contest at the pool.

This trophy has been won by members of the Army Cadets, pictured outside the Drill Hall on Barton Road. The Cambridgeshire Regiment badge adorns the building, which was opened in May 1939 by Gen. R.M. Luckock, a native of Ely.

Miss Mary Butcher and pupils at the Broad Street School. It closed in 1968.

In May 1961 the Hospital Sunday parade was revived, and proved a great success. The Round Table float, a Roman chariot hauled by captive Britons, is seen in West End.

Midway along the route the procession stopped at St Mary's Green, where a united service was held. Altogether the parade raised over £200 for the Friends of the Tower and St John's Hospitals.

Section Four

DRAINING &

FLOODING

Looking towards the railway bridge across the swollen River Ouse, January 1928.

The Overfall Mill, which threw water with its scoopwheel from Middle Fen Drain into the Ouse. Enlarged in 1792, it was finally demolished in 1917, although the sails had been removed some years earlier. The height of the mill is indicated by the size of the people standing near it.

The Cross family ran and lived in the mill for several generations, and this interior view, probably dating from the early 1900s, shows how fine a home it made.

The caption on this postcard reads 'Duck shooting in the Fens, the start'. Robert Cross sits in his gunning boat holding his punt gun, on the drain side of the mill.

The wind was not a reliable source of power, and from the beginning of the nineteenth century steam engines took on the task of draining the fens. At Prickwillow two engine houses were built: the one on the right in 1831 and the other in 1880.

The first steam engine drove a scoopwheel, and the second drove a centrifugal pump. This interior of the 1880 engine house shows part of the beam engine.

Besides a competent engineer the steam engines needed fuel, and here coal is being unloaded from a barge at the quay in Prickwillow.

Steam power was itself superseded by diesel power, and this engine house was built on the site of the Overfall Mill to house a three-cylinder Mirrlees marine engine. It was last operated in 1971.

This five-cylinder Mirrlees diesel engine replaced the 1880 steam engine at Prickwillow, and was officially 'opened' in December 1924. At the time diesel fuel was less than half the cost of coal.

Not only does the pumping machinery need to be efficient, the drainage channels themselves have to be regularly maintained. Here a dyker proudly displays his skill and his tools, 1890s.

Before widespread mechanisation, the larger the drain, the more men were employed. This gang is at work in the Engine Drain at Prickwillow.

This early dragline, manufactured by Priestman Bros, could be bought for £1,575, and a special feature of the latest model was the driver's seat! It is slubbing out White Wing Drain, near Swasedale Drove, with the Old Bank behind.

The river banks and channels also need to be maintained, and here workmen employed by the Burnt Fen Commissioners are busy on the bank of the River Lark at Prickwillow, 1890s.

Gault, the clay used for strengthening the banks, was dug from the Roswell Pits and transported by barge to where it was needed. Here a gaulter empties his wheelbarrow into a barge, after a precarious journey along one of the plank walkways.

Centuries of digging have changed what was once Roswell Hill into Roswell Pits. Gaulters are at work in the middle distance, and the sugar-beet factory is beyond, 1930s.

A dredger working from a barge on the River Lark, 1930. Bridge Farm, Prickwillow, is on the right.

Ely High Bridge and station at the turn of the century. The Wash is in flood, and the chains and posts provide a necessary guide for the wary traveller.

Annesdale and the Cutter Inn menaced by flood water, January 1928. High water levels in Ely were a regular occurrence, until major river improvements were made after the floods of 1947. A new cut-off channel was dug along the eastern edge of the Fens, and the river banks were heightened.

Swans take advantage of the flood, while the cottage on Babylon aptly demonstrates why fewer people were willing to live across the water, March 1937.

In March 1947 the Fens suffered severe flooding, and had the banks not given way elsewhere the situation in Ely could have been even worse than this.

The River Lark in flood at Prickwillow, 1912. The Anchor public house is surrounded by flood water, but, as the washing on the line demonstrates, life goes on!

Next door to the Anchor was the Forge. As there was no upstairs to retreat to, it had to be abandoned. The pumping engines in the village ran night and day for three weeks without stopping.

Prickwillow post office and shop threatened by flood water, 1937. Compare this view with that on page 117 to see the more usual river level.

The hastily erected bank looks barely up to the task, with so much water behind it.

A locomotive approaches the station with The Wash in full flood. In March 1947 conditions in the Fens were unequalled by anything within living memory.

The approach to Ely High Bridge providing a good vantage point for the curious. On 16 March at the height of the gale it was said to resemble a sea-side promenade at high tide on a very rough day.

Looking south from the west tower of the cathedral over the station to the Newmarket railway line.

The 'Battle of the Banks' became a military operation, with hundreds of soldiers and German prisoners of war being brought in to help. In the Bell Hotel army officers and a BBC film crew discuss the day's events. The immediate plan appears to be to drink the place dry!

Soldiers from the army camp off West Fen Road setting off to help, under the watchful eye of an NCO.

Brothers in adversity. Fenmen, British soldiers and German prisoners of war all fought day after day, night after night, against the common enemy.

Section Five

THE VILLAGES
WITHIN THE CITY

Stuntney, June 1933. James Bullock of the Cambridge Antiquarian Society sets
up his camera and tripod near the Anchor public house.

Quanea Farm, *c*. 1927. Bob Chapman and Liles Human are standing in front of the horse and cart, with Florence Cox behind, and her son Tom on the horse.

Laburnum House, off Stuntney Causeway, March 1933. The winter condition of a fen drove is shown in the foreground.

Stuntney Old Hall, 1926. The manor passed from the Steward family to Oliver Cromwell in 1636. At the time of this photograph it was owned by O. Ambrose, who lived in the 'new' hall, a quarter of a mile away. This had been built because the Old Hall was falling down.

Lower Street, looking towards the post office, June 1933.

Holy Cross Church, built in 1876 and restored in 1903. Little of the Norman church it replaced was incorporated in the new building.

Children take part in a church parade, led by a band, 1909.

St Michael's and All Angels' Church, Chettisham. This twelfth- and thirteenth-century building has not been quite so drastically restored as Stuntney Church.

Chettisham School, winners of the Isle of Ely attendance shield in 1922. The school was built in 1880, enlarged in 1897 and closed in 1934.

Queen Adelaide, *c.* 1900. Beyond the pump is the school house, the school, and two of the three level-crossings in the village.

St Etheldreda's Church and the post office, *c.* 1905. Erected in 1883, the former was sold for conversion into a private dwelling in 1978.

The public house from which the village took its name, 1930. In the background the new river bridge is under construction.

The ancient Plough public house, Old Bank which was catered for river traffic held up at shallows on the River Ouse, was itself left high and dry when the river was diverted in 1830. It is now a private house, the origins of this late fifteenth- or early sixteenth-century building are obscure.

The old house seen on the right, through the steel frame of the sugar-beet factory, was the last link with the ancient manor of Turbutsey. The manor was given to monks by a charter of 1109.

Workmen engaged in building the weighbridge bungalow at the entrance to the factory. Memories of military service are still fresh.

The factory took a year to build, and was opened in October 1925. Beet came by rail, road and river. The factory eventually closed in 1981.

Part of the factory's large fleet of barges. Standing on the tug is Ben Lee. He lived in one of a number of houseboats moored on the river at Queen Adelaide.

A church Sunday School group, 1890s.

Children at Queen Adelaide School, 1920s. Built to accommodate fifty pupils, it was opened in 1872, enlarged in 1885 and closed in 1953.

This portrait was taken in the school yard to mark the enrolment of the first Girl Guide group in the village, April 1940.

Harry Cross, foreman of Wades Farm, with a happy gang of Land Army girls.

Adelaide FC, winners of the Isle Lower Junior Cup, 1930. Back row, left to right: Claude Oxer, Claude Cross, Joe Wren, George Dockerill, -?-. Middle row: Maurice Wright, Fred Needham, Arthur Cross. Front row: Ernie Dockerill, Bert Clark, Stan Hopkin, Felix Cross, Horrie Fowler.

Canoeing on the River Ouse. It was here, between Littleport and Adelaide bridge, that the 1944 Oxford and Cambridge boat race was held. Five thousand people saw Oxford win by three-quarters of a length!

St James's Church, Burnt Fen. This mission church, made of corrugated iron, was built to serve the more remote parts of Prickwillow parish. It was dedicated on 25 November 1890.

The church interior. In March 1895 a terrific gale badly damaged the building. It was subsequently repaired.

Lady cyclists outside Burnt Fen School. The school opened in 1870. By 1932 it had become so overcrowded that the newly erected Institute was used to accommodate some children. The school closed in 1961.

A catechism group from St James's, 1909. Claude Kingdon was curate and then vicar of Prickwillow for a total of thirty-five years.

Hanslip Long, second from the right, watching game being boxed at Shippea Hill, *c.* 1900. He farmed here for more than forty years.

An accident involving the Norwich express, near Shippea Hill station, 7 April 1906. The line had recently undergone repairs. The station name had not long been changed from Burnt Fen, which residents had felt detracted from the value of their produce!

A boarded and thatched cottage opposite Burnt Fen School at the end of the last century.

Burnt Fen Institute, opened by Sir Fred Hiam in 1932. The inset shows the Revd W. Francis Hicks and Mr and Mrs A. Crust, 'each of whom devoted a large number of hours to making the Institute an accomplished fact'.

Celery planting on the Letter F Farm, Mildenhall Road, 1941. Horses were still very much involved in farm work, although one tractor is being used.

The dropping and dibbing in of thousands of plants was a back-breaking job.

Prickwillow from the bank of the River Lark, *c.* 1905. There were toll-gates on either side of the bridge to raise money for the upkeep of the river banks.

The river bridge decorated for Queen Victoria's Diamond Jubilee, 1897. Another arch is visible below the pumping engine chimney.

Main Street from the bridge, *c*. 1900. Until 1830 the River Ouse had joined the Lark here. The road remained on the former river bank above the neighbouring houses, and the church, school and other buildings to the north of this were built on the old river bed.

The village pump, which supplied water directly from the river, *c*. 1900. In front, reading the newspaper, is Alfred Beazley. The toll-house is behind.

Barges at the quay near the two pumping-engine houses. On the right is the original shop and post office. This was owned by the Edwards family, who came to the village in 1856.

By about 1915 a new house and an extension had been added to the shop. Albert Edwards, who died in 1945 aged seventy-nine, was sub-postmaster here for some fifty years.

Main Street, *c.* 1927. The large iron pipes on the right, near the commissioners' hut (see p. 88), had come from the pumping engine. They were taken away for scrap during the Second World War.

Members of the Anchor Share-out Benefit Club, pose outside the Anchor with their decorated float, Hospital Sunday, 1924. Olive Edwards and Florence Mott are the nurses, and Tootsie Croll is the patient. A total of £84 was collected for Addenbrooke's Hospital, Cambridge.

St Peter's Church, 1890s. It replaced an earlier building erected in 1849, which had served as both church and school. The new church was consecrated in 1866.

The new parish of Prickwillow was formed in 1878 and extended across the Fens into Norfolk and Suffolk. On 25 September that year the Bishop of Ely ceremonially drove in the first pile to support the new vicarage. Seen here standing at the gate is the Revd J.K.C. Payne, *c.* 1927.

The school decorated for the Coronation, 1937. In May the children had been prevented from taking part in the celebrations because of a measles epidemic. They had to wait until the end of June for their tea, parade and sports.

There had been no problems two years before in May 1935, when these children sat down to a meal in the school to celebrate George V's Silver Jubilee.

A different generation of Prickwillow children poses with Miss Eva Cross in the school playground, September 1950. The school had opened in 1862; it closed in 1984.

Pausing for water, or refreshment of a different type, the crew of a steam lorry stops at the Waggon and Horses. The lorry is carrying Fen produce to London.

The ex-Servicemen's Institute decorated for the Coronation, 1937. A branch of the British Legion had been formed in Prickwillow in 1932, and in December 1933 this building opened as both their headquarters and as a community hall.

Main Street, looking towards St Peter's Church, the Waggon and Horses and the Baptist chapel, at the beginning of the century. Both the Baptists and the Methodists had organised congregations and chapels here before the first Anglican church was built.

The Ely Road entrance to the village, decorated with an arch for Queen Victoria's Jubilee, 1897. Jeremiah Taylor's house and shop can be seen through the arch. It was severely damaged by fire in January 1955, and then demolished.

Main Street, showing Taylor's Stores on the right. *c.* 1927.

The entrance to the Old Bank Road, *c.* 1927. The former river bank, following the old course of the River Ouse and marking the boundary between Middle Fen and Padnal Fen, was not cleared away until 1973.

Schoolboys watch the photographer, Ely Road, *c.* 1927. In the foreground is The Limes farm, and beyond Mill Villa is the flour mill. Its chimney had fallen in the gale of 1895.

British Legion members on parade at the unveiling of the war memorial on Armistice Sunday, 1947. Walter Brand, the standard-bearer, had served in the Suffolk Regiment during the First World War, and the names of at least twelve of his comrades were engraved on the memorial. They were among the twenty-seven from Prickwillow who died.

Members of the Prickwillow Amateur Swimming Club beside the River Lark, with instructors Eddie Scott, Eddie Bullingham and Jack Bavey, 1948.

Competitors in a baby show held in the vicarage garden, September 1929. The judge, Dr G.B. Davis, is seen with (among others) members of the Benton, Bonnett, Brown, Dew, Fitch, Fletcher, Gooch, Jakes, Leggett, Skipper and Thorpe families.

An infant welfare party in the Institute, 1954. District nurses C.M. Biart and K. Railton are pictured with helpers, mothers and children.

ACKNOWLEDGEMENTS

The principal acknowledgement is to Cambridgeshire Libraries and Heritage, Cambridgeshire County Council, for permission to use photographs held in the Cambridgeshire Collection.

A significant part of that collection is the photographic archive of the Cambridge Antiquarian Society, and I would like to thank the society and its Honorary Librarian, John Pickles, for permission to use items from this.

I would like to mention my colleagues in the Cambridgeshire Collection, who work so hard to collect material from the county's past and present for the future, particularly Fiona Parish and Katherine Heawood, with whom it is a pleasure to work. A special thanks must go to my colleague and former Ely Librarian Lynda Martin, for her encouragement, enthusiasm, and help in compiling this volume. I must also mention the two photographers whom the collection uses, Les Goodey and Ed Collinson.

Many people have given photographs to the Cambridgeshire Collection, or loaned them for copying, and many others have allowed me to copy views of Prickwillow. The following is a list of those whose photographs or knowledge has contributed to this volume. I am grateful to them all, and I apologise to anyone I may have omitted:

P. Blakeman • T. Cox • E. Cross • T. Day • D. Dockerill • Ely Museum
R. Howe • F. Jakes • O. Jakes • P. Lawrence • R. Lee • T. Lee • J. Line
D. Morbey • R. Neal • M. Pearce • M. Rouse • E. Scott • R. Scott
K. Stacey • D. Walsh

Other titles published by The History Press

Ely Then and Now
PAMELA BLAKEMAN

This book is part of the Then & Now series, which matches old photographs with modern ones taken from the same camera locations, to demonstrate the changes that have occurred over the years. The images include streets, buildings, people, and social activities in each local area.

978-0-7524-2652-5

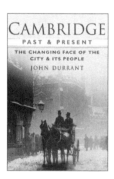

Cambridge Past and Present
JOHN DURRANT

Cows rather than cars on New Square - images of Cambridge in the early 20th century, set alongside photographs of the same locations in 2000, make for an engrossing study of the city. The pictures are accompanied by informative captions by an expert on Cambridge's planning and progress, former mayor John Durrant.

978-0-7509-4908-8

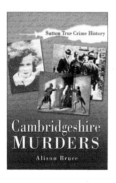

Cambridgeshire Murders
TED GOSLING

The county's most fascinating crimes: from the mysterious barn fire at Burwell that killed 76 people to the unsolved murder of Cambridge shopkeeper Alice Lawton, this is a collection of the county's most dramatic and interesting criminal cases. Alison Bruce has gone back to original records and documents to uncover the truth about these extraordinary crimes.

978-0-7509-3914-0

Visit our website and discover thousands of other History Press books.
www.thehistorypress.co.uk